North American Indians Today

Apache

Cherokee

Cheyenne

Comanche

Creek

Crow

Huron

Iroquois

Navajo

Ojibwa

Osage

Potawatomi

Pueblo

Seminole

Sioux

North American
Indians Today

Creek

by
Autumn Libal

Mason Crest Publishers

Philadelphia

The author wishes to thank the Creek Council House Museum, the Muscogee Nation of Oklahoma, and the Poarch Band of Creek Indians. Special thanks to A.D. Ellis, Dana Tiger, Don Blair, Eddie Tullis, Joyce A. Bear, Mal D. McGhee, Roy Shivers, Ted Isham, Timothy Ramer, Wilbur Gouge, and all the other people who generously contributed their time and knowledge to this book.

Mason Crest Publishers Inc.
370 Reed Road
Broomall, Pennsylvania 19008
(866) MCP-BOOK (toll free)

First printing
1 2 3 4 5 6 7 8 9 10
Library of Congress Cataloging-in-Publication Data on file at the Library of Congress.
ISBN: 1-59084-668-0
1-59084-663-X (series)

Design by Lori Holland.
Composition by Bytheway Publishing Services, Binghamton, New York.
Cover design by Benjamin Stewart.
Printed and bound in the Hashemite Kingdom of Jordan.
Photography by Benjamin Stewart. Artwork on pp. 22, 64, 72, 76, 77, 78, 79, 80, 82 courtesy of Dana Tiger. Photos on pp. 35, 58, 59, 60, 84, 88 courtesy of the Poarch Creek Tribe. Art on p. 6 by Keith Rosco.

Contents

Why is it so important that Indians be brought into the "mainstream" of American life?
I would not know how to interpret this phrase to my people.
The closest I would be able to come would be "a big wide river".
Am I then to tell my people that they are to be thrown into the big, wide river of the United States?

Earl Old Person
Blackfeet Tribal Chairman

Introduction

In the midst of twenty-first–century North America, how do the very first North Americans hold on to their unique cultural identity? At the same time, how do they adjust to the real demands of the modern world? Earl Old Person's quote on the opposite page expresses the difficulty of achieving this balance. Even the common values of the rest of North America—like fitting into the "mainstream"—may seem strange or undesireable to North American Indians. How can these groups of people thrive and prosper in the twenty-first century without losing their traditions, the ways of thinking and living that have been handed down to them by their ancestors? How can they keep from drowning in North America's "big, wide river"?

Thoughts from the Series Consultant

Each of the books in this series was written with the help of Native scholars and tribal leaders from the particular tribe. Based on oral histories as well as written documents, these books describe the current strategies of each Native nation to develop its economy while maintaining strong ties with its culture. As a result, you may find that these books read far differently from other books about Native Americans.

Over the past centuries, Native groups have faced increasing pressure to conform to the wishes of the governments that took their lands. Often brutally inhumane methods were implemented to change Native social systems. These books describe the ways that Native groups refused to be passive recipients of change, even in the face of these past atrocities. Heroic individuals worked to fit external changes into local conditions. This struggle continues today.

The legacy of the past still haunts the psyche of both Native and non-Native people of North America; hopefully, these books will help correct some misunderstandings. And even with the difficulties encountered by past and current Native leaders, Native nations continue to thrive. As this series illustrates, Native populations continue to increase—and they have clearly persevered against incredible odds. North American culture's big, wide river may be deep and cold—but Native Americans are good swimmers!

—Martha McCollough

Breaking Stereotypes

One way that some North Americans may "drown" Native culture is by using stereotypes to think about North American Indians. When we use stereotypes to think about a group of people, we assume things about them because of their race or cultural group. Instead of taking time to understand individual differences and situations, we lump together everyone in a certain group. In reality, though, every person is different. More than two million Native people live in North America, and they are as *diverse* as any other group. Each one is unique.

Even if we try hard to avoid stereotypes, however, it isn't always easy to know what words to use. Should we call the people who are native to North America Native Americans—or American Indians—or just Indians?

The word "Indian" probably comes from a mistake—when Christopher Columbus arrived in the New World, he thought he had reached India, so he called the people he found there Indians. Some people feel it doesn't make much sense to call Native Americans "Indians." (Suppose Columbus had thought he landed in China instead of India; would we today call Native people "Chinese"?) Other scholars disagree; for example, Russell Means, Native politician and activist, claims that the word "Indian" comes from Columbus saying the native people were *en Dios*—"in God," or naturally spiritual.

Many Canadians use the term "First Nations" to refer to the Native peoples who live there, and people in the United States usually speak of Native Americans. Most Native people we talked to while we were writing these books prefer the simple term "Indian"—or they would rather use the names of their tribes. (We have used the term "North American Indians" for our series to distinguish this group of people from the inhabitants of India.)

Even the definition of what makes a person "Indian" varies. The U.S. government recognizes certain groups as tribal nations (almost 500 in all). Each nation then decides how it will enroll people as members of that tribe. Tribes may require a particular amount of Indian blood, tribal membership of the father or the mother, or other *criteria*. Some enrolled tribal members who are legally "Indian" may not look Native at all; many have blond hair and blue eyes and others have clearly African features. At the same time, there are thousands of Native people whose tribes have not yet been officially recognized by the government.

We have done our best to write books that are as free from stereotypes as possible. But you as the reader also play a part. After reading one of these books, we hope you won't think: "The Cheyenne are all like this" or "Iroquois are all like that." Each person in this world is unique, whatever their culture. Stereotypes shut people's minds—but these books are intended to open your mind. North American Indians today have much wisdom and beauty to offer.

Some people consider American Indians to be a historical topic only, but Indians today are living, contributing members of North American society. The contributions of the various Indian cultures enrich our world—and North America would be a very different place without the Native people who live there. May they never be lost in North America's "big, wide river"!

The fog was thick like sadness and the people wandered frightened and alone.

Chapter 1

History:
From Emergence to
the Trail of Tears

Long ago, when the world was still new, there was a small hole in the backbone of the earth. The people crawled out of this hole like ants and lived where the tan mountains stretched up to touch the sky.

In this long-ago time, Esakitaummesee, the Master of Breath, sent a fog over the whole earth. The fog was thick like sadness and wet like dew. The People could not see, for the fog was in their eyes like tears. They wandered through the fog, frightened and alone, calling out to each other with hesitant voices.

Sometimes a Person bumped into another Person in the fog, and then they held onto each other like ghosts hold on to the world. Despair filled their hearts, and they cried to the Master of Breath to have mercy on their loneliness and suffering.

The Master of Breath heard the people crying, and the sound was sad to him, so he went to the place where the sun rises and began to blow. The

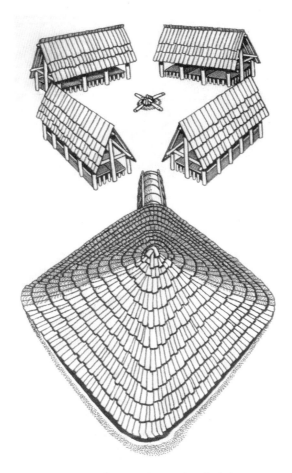

Traditional Muscogee ceremonial grounds consisted of the ceremonial fire, four arbors, and a large chokkova (or council house). The arbors faced the cardinal directions: north, east, south, and west.

fog rippled and rolled. Pushed by the Master's breath, it dipped into valleys and billowed over mountains until the final tattered ribbons of it were swept away. As the fog lifted from the people's eyes, a new world was revealed to them, and they raised their voices, not in frightened cries, but in joyous songs of thanksgiving to the Master of Breath.

That day, the People looked at those they had grasped in the fog and embraced each other out of love instead of fear. The groups who had found each other in the fog promised to live together always as brothers and sisters, mothers and fathers to each other. The People who were closest to the east, the first to see the sun, praised the Master of Breath for blowing away the fog and called themselves the Wind Clan. Another group of People saw an alligator as the fog blew away, so they became the Alligator Clan. The People who saw a bear became the Bear Clan. One group looked up toward the sky and saw a bird flying through the fogless air and called themselves the Bird Clan. And so each group of People took the name of the first animal, plant, or natural element that was revealed to them out of the fog.

Then the Master of Breath spoke to the People. He said, "You are the beginning of each one of your families and clans. Live up to your name. Never eat of your own clan, for it is your brother. Never marry into your own clan. Such a marriage will destroy you. Young men, when you marry, move with your wife, and raise your children in her clan. Do these things, and you will be a powerful People. Forget, and the People will die."

This is how the clans came to be, and this is how they are still today.

Long before television and flight, before kings and queens, before the Vikings and Christianity, long before there were books or even written words, people lived on the continent that is now called North America. No one knows how many people once lived in these vast lands, but we do

Muscogee or Muskokee?

If you look in books or on the Internet, you will find the word Muscogee spelled in many different ways. In the Muscogean language, Muscogee is spelled *Mvskoke*. However, the many different English spellings of the word probably come from the fact that Europeans spelled the word phonetically, the way the word sounded. If you search for this word on the Internet, you will find it spelled: Muscogee, Muskogee, Muskokee, Mvskoke, Mvskokee, Muskoki and perhaps other spellings as well. But don't be fooled. Each of these words refers to the Muscogee people or to the language that they speak.

This historical drawing portrays a Muscogee man in formal dress that mixes Muscogean and European fashions. Members of Southeastern tribes often wore turbans. When Europeans took Native Americans to Europe, they dressed them in the outfits of their slaves and servants. Turbans were part of this dress, and the style was brought back and made popular in North America.

know that great civilizations with complex *economies*, intricate governments, and diverse cultures thrived in the *Western Hemisphere* for thousands of years before Columbus and other Europeans came and claimed
this land as their own.

One of the groups who lived on this continent long before Europeans
came was the Muscogee. According to tradition, the Muscogee people
originally lived in the Southwest, but migrated to the Southeast where they
settled throughout the land that is now called Georgia and Alabama. Early
Muscogee ancestors built huge mound buildings. These impressive earthen
pyramids were part of their ceremonial grounds. Though the architecture,
dwellings, and ceremonial grounds of the Muscogee people have changed,
the pyramids their ancestors built are still greatly *revered*.

In the southeastern lands, the Muscogee were *agriculturalists* who built
their towns near waterways where the soil was rich for farming and where
game was plentiful. When Europeans came to these southeastern lands,
they called the Muscogee people "Creeks," because their towns were built
along creeks and rivers. Today, the use of the term Creek is so *pervasive*
that most *non-Native* people do not even know that the true tribal name is
Muscogee.

Rather than being a single tribe, the Muscogee people were actually a
confederacy of more than one hundred tribal towns. Each tribal town had
its own community, leaders, and chief. The chiefs of all the tribal towns
would meet to discuss matters that affected the whole confederacy. When
the Muscogee fought and defeated other tribes, those tribes were invited to
join the confederacy as new tribal towns.

The center of each town had a plaza for dancing and ceremonies and
two buildings for council meetings. One building was round and enclosed
for winter meetings. The other building was open, with a roof but no walls,
for meeting in the hot summer months. In a similar way, families often had
two houses: an open building for the summer and a closed building with a
shingled roof for the winter. The large, central town was called a *talwa*.
Outside of the talwa were *talofa*, or smaller villages. Today, many people
think that all North American Indians were *transient* people who always
moved from place to place, but this was not the case for the Muscogee or
many other Native people. The Muscogee towns, homes, and farms were
well-established, permanent, and productive communities.

Most of the confederacy's growth came from the expansion of its towns
into "mother" and "daughter" towns. When a tribal town grew to between

four hundred and six hundred people, approximately half the town would split off to build a new town somewhere nearby. When creating the new town, the tribal members would take embers from the mother talwa's fire to start the fire of the daughter town. The daughter talwa would build its own ceremonial grounds and council buildings, elect its own chief, and have its own villages and fields for farming. The transfer of fire from the mother talwa to the daughter talwa represented the great unity of the Muscogee Confederacy. When an outside tribe joined the confederacy, they would also receive fire from one of the tribal towns.

The clan system also helped to create harmony and *interrelations* within the nation. Muscogee people identified themselves by the clan, or family group, to which they belonged. Most towns would have many clans within them. Because the Muscogee are a *matrilineal* people, clan membership is passed down through the mother's side of the family. Everyone within a clan is considered family, so marrying within your clan is strictly forbidden.

When two people got married, the man left his family and clan and went to live with his wife's family. Their children would be members of the mother's clan. The close relationships that developed through marriage between clans and towns were good for the overall peace and harmony of the confederacy. Just like today, many people lived, raised children, and died in the towns where they were born . . . until the governments of the European powers and the United States changed all that.

The first contact the Muscogee had with Europeans probably came between 1539 and 1543 when the Spanish *conquistador* Hernando de Soto arrived in what the Europeans called the "New World." De Soto came with six hundred soldiers, two hundred *cavalry* men, dogs trained to *disembowel* people, and a *mandate* from the Spanish government to seize any land and wealth he found for Spain. In four short years, De Soto sliced and fought his way through hundreds of miles of land, leaving death and disease in his wake.

In the late 1600s under pressure from the British, the Muscogee were forced to *relinquish* the first of their lands in Georgia. As the Muscogee moved westward, the groups that settled along the Chattahoochee and Flint (Thronateeskee) Rivers became known as the Lower Creeks, and the groups that settled along the Coosa and Tallapoosa Rivers became known as the Upper Creeks. What began as a geographical division between Upper Creeks and Lower Creeks, however, would one day grow to be a major political and military division of the Muscogee Confederacy.

Through the 1700s, the British extended their reach over Native lands by establishing a colony in what is now Georgia. The Muscogee Nation was under ever-increasing pressure from the British to the north and east, the Spanish to the south, and the French to the west. Over the years, numerous treaties were signed by the Muscogee attempting to maintain peaceful relations with the Europeans who were closing in on all sides.

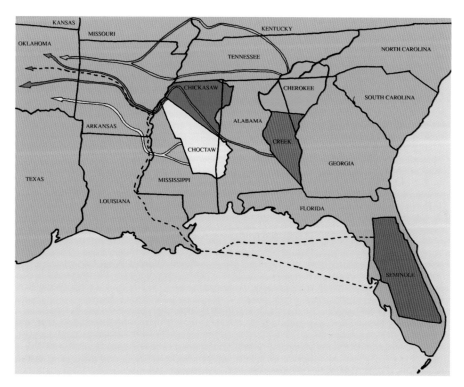

During the Trail of Tears, the native people of the Southeastern lands were forced across a number of land and water routes to Indian Territory. No matter which route they took, they met starvation, hardship, and death along the way.

Some treaties were meant to establish meaningful trade with the Europeans, trade that could benefit the Muscogee Nation's economy. Other treaties gave the Europeans portions of the Muscogee lands. The Europeans often used false promises (such as offering goods, services, or military protection that would never appear) combined with the threat of their overwhelming military force to **coerce** the Muscogee people into signing these treaties. Throughout the century, the Europeans steadily **encroached**

Clans of the Muscogee Confederacy

Hanging on the wall of the Seminole Nation Museum in Wewoka, Oklahoma, is the following record of clans of the Muskokee Confederacy. The names in bold are those clans that still survive:

Alligator	Fox	Rabbit
Arrow	Grass	**Raccoon**
Bear	Hair	Raven
Beaver	Hickory Nut	Red Paint
Bird	Horned Owl	Salt
Buffalo	Land	**Skunk**
Buzzard	**Lye**	**Snake**
Cane	Medicine	Spanish
Corn	Mink	Toad
Crow	Mole	Turkey
Daddy Longlegs	Moss	**Turtle**
Deer	Muskrat	**Water Moccasin**
Dew	**Otter**	Weevil
Eagle	**Panther**	Wildcat
Earth	**Potato**	**Wind**
Fish	Pumpkin	Wolf

Probably no one knows how many clans existed in the Muscogee Confederacy before the Europeans came to North America, but we do know that very few survived to the present day.

upon Muscogee lands, taking them piece-by-piece. But even if some in the Muscogee Nation felt things could not get any worse, even more changes, with their devastating consequences, were yet to come.

In 1775 through 1783, the European settlers on the eastern coast of what is now the United States fought Great Britain for independence. During the Revolutionary War, the official policy of the Muscogee Nation was to remain neutral. Great Britain's loss

> "On no account whatever will we consent to sell one foot of our land, neither by exchange or otherwise; this talk is not only to last during the life of our present chiefs, but to their descendants after them."
>
> —Menawa, Creek, 1824

in the war created new problems for the Muscogee Nation and for all the native tribes. With independence, the settlers no longer saw themselves as Europeans or foreigners in a foreign land. Now they saw themselves as owners of the land. Because many of them had been born in the colonies, they even began to see themselves as "natives" of the land. Their colonies became states with independent governments. Europe was no longer their home; America was their home; and instead of seeing themselves as the invaders of the Indian's land, they saw the Indians as invaders of the new "American" land.

In 1811, Chief Tecumseh of the Shawnee came to the Muscogee Nation in his quest to unite all Native Americans in a *pan-Indian* movement. Tecumseh believed that if the Native people did not work together, the tribes would be conquered one by one until the U.S. government controlled everything and all the tribes disappeared. However, he believed that if the tribes united, they could overwhelm the young United States and reclaim all that had been taken from them. Stirred by Tecumseh, the Muscogee National Council passed a law forbidding the sale of tribal land. The punishment for any person breaking this tribal law would be death.

Despite Tecumseh's convincing arguments for a pan-Indian movement and constant pressure from white settlers, the Muscogee Nation could not unite against the American government. In 1812, the United States again declared war against the British, this time fighting to the north in Canada and to the south in Florida. Tecumseh and those who had joined the pan-Indian movement, including the Upper Creeks, joined forces with the British, hoping to cripple or even overthrow the U.S. government. However, a smaller part of the Muscogee Nation, the Lower Creeks, believed that siding with the new American government would ultimately be more *advantageous*, so they joined the American forces. The Lower Creeks and Upper Creeks ended up fighting against each other, and when the War of 1812 was over, deep divisions remained in the Muscogee Nation.

In 1825, William McIntosh, one of the chiefs of the Lower Creeks, signed a treaty with the U.S. government giving all Lower Creek lands to the United States. McIntosh and those who acted with him, however, did not have the power to sign such a treaty without the approval of the entire Muscogee Nation, and since the nation had already passed a law against the sale of tribal lands, the treaty was illegal. The punishment for sale of tribal lands was death, so a group of Red Sticks (or warriors) was sent to carry out the death sentences of Chief McIntosh and the other leaders responsible for the loss of lands. Nevertheless, by 1827, the Muscogee people no longer held any land in Georgia, and their original southeastern lands were reduced to an area of what is now Alabama.

In 1829, Andrew Jackson's *inauguration* as the seventh president of the United States marked the end of life in the Southeast for the Muscogee Nation and for all Native people. When Jackson ran for president, he used his intention to drive all Indians to the west of the Mississippi River as a major

The Weapons of Invasion

When the Europeans came to North America, their greatest weapons against the Native people turned out not to be swords but diseases. In Europe, people were exposed to numerous diseases, such as smallpox, dysentery, cholera, the common cold, and flu. These diseases never existed in North America before the Europeans came, so the Native people had no natural immunity. Even Europeans who did not appear sick carried diseases that proved deadly to the Muscogee and to all Native people. No one knows how many Native people lived in North and South America before Europeans came to these continents. What we do know is that the death toll from these European diseases was in the millions.

The Muscogee people are matrilineal. This is not at all unusual among Native people, not only in North America but all over the world as well. In contrast, most North American and Western cultures are patrilineal, meaning that family membership is traced through the father's side. Think about your family. Does your last name come from your father, from your mother, or from both?

element of his *campaign platform*. In 1830, Congress passed and Jackson signed the Indian Removal Act into law, paving the way for all Southeast Indians who refused to give up their Native identity to be removed. Under President Jackson's plan, the Indians would be forced to march overland to "Indian Territory."

The "Trail of Tears" is a name that was given to the one-thousand mile (1,700-kilometer) march the Muscogee, Cherokee, Seminole, Choctaw, and Chickasaw Nations made from the southeastern United States to what is now Oklahoma. Tens of thousands were forced to make this brutal march, which took a full month to cross the Mississippi River alone. Much of the march took place in the winter months. Food was scarce, the people had no shelter, and disease spread quickly. Parents had to carry their small children, and many of the elderly fell behind. When the survivors arrived in Oklahoma, their tears and their thousands of dead stretched out for one thousand miles behind them.

When the Muscogee people were forced to Indian Territory, they brought their council fires with them. Dana Tiger's painting Keeping Cultures Fire Burning *emphasizes the importance of women as keepers of native culture.*

Chapter 2

The Muscogee Nation: From Relocation to Today

The land is flat and somehow mysterious. Where your feet stand, the earth used to shake beneath great stampedes of buffalo. Here, heads tossing and tails lifting into the wind, herds of mustangs galloped across the plains. Small, tunnel-shaped dust storms and towering, vicious tornadoes rage through this land. Out on the horizon, a great earthen pyramid rises from the flat earth toward the vast, open sky.

It could be one of the ancient mound buildings of old, where people gathered for their most sacred celebrations. But the cars, trucks, and SUVs parked out front tell you it is not. You walk through the dark, swinging doors and step into the light to see offices equipped with computers and people filing paperwork at their desks. There is a great auditorium where hundreds can gather for meetings. Down the hall is a modern courtroom where judges preside over important hearings. This building is not an ancient remnant of a lost civilization. It is one of the most important government buildings of the modern-day Muscogee Nation. Located in Okmulgee, Oklahoma, this great mound building is a sign of *continuity* with the past—and it also indicates the Muscogee Nation's undying presence today.

The descendents of those Creek people who survived the Trail of Tears make up today's Muscogee Nation. However, the troubles the Muscogee people faced in the Southeast did not end when they arrived in Indian Territory. Here the lies and broken promises of the U.S. government—and the greed of settlers and fortune hunters—continued to plague the Muscogee people. Then, with the start of the American Civil War, the Muscogee people found their lives devastated once more by a battle that was not their own.

Caught squarely between the army of the North and the army of the South, *neutrality* seemed impossible for the Muscogee Nation. When the Southern Confederacy signed a treaty with the Creek Nation, those Creeks

This government building in Okmulgee, Oklahoma, reminds the Muscogee people of the great mound buildings constructed by their ancestors. It stands as a striking connection between the people of the present and the traditions of the past.

When Things Aren't What They Seem

In 1934, Congress passed the Indian Reorganization Act allowing tribes to once again establish their own tribal governments. On its surface, this decision makes it look like the U.S. government was trying to treat the Native Americans more fairly. However, the Indian Reorganization Act is an example of how some things are not always as they seem. Congress made sure that the Act applied to all states except Oklahoma. However, in 1934, almost all federally recognized tribes were located within the state of Oklahoma, so in reality, the act changed nothing for Native people because the tribes were not located where they could take advantage of the new law. By enacting such a law, the federal government was able to make it look like it was making positive reforms while in reality it was just maintaining the status quo. Two years after passage of the Indian Reorganization Act, a second act was passed to apply to the Native peoples in Oklahoma.

who had favored neutrality marched with those who supported the U.S. government's position to Kansas where they joined the **Union**. When the Union won the Civil War, the U.S. government punished the Creek Nation (including those who fought on the Union side) by seizing large tracts of land in Indian Territory.

In 1887, the U.S. government decided that the best way to deal with tribal land disputes and rid themselves of the "problem" of the Indian Nations would be to take away all tribal lands and give the land to individuals. Such an arrangement was in the U.S. government's best interest, because when tribal lands were sold, the whole tribe had to agree to the sale and a treaty had to be approved by the tribal government. If individuals owned the land, however, those individuals could sell the land without the tribe's approval. Under the Dawes Act, Muscogee lands in Oklahoma were divided and *parceled* out in 160-acre (65-hectare) *allotments* to individual families.

Many Native people supported the Dawes Act, because they thought it would give them ownership of their land once and for all. However, at the same time that the government was dividing the land among the Indians in Oklahoma, they were opening up all unclaimed land to settlers in what is now called the "Great Land Rush." Additionally, in 1891, President Benjamin Harrison ordered that 900,000 acres (364,500 hectares) of the Indian

The Great Seal of the Muscogee Nation features a plow and golden shafts of wheat to symbolize their agriculturalist roots.

lands in Oklahoma be opened up to white settlers. Many of the Indians who received land under the Dawes Act were in such desperate poverty that they were forced to turn around and almost immediately sell their land in order to have money to survive. By the time land allotments were complete in Oklahoma, a book had been published showing the land allotments and giving the names of the people who owned them. The existence of this book made it easy for **oil speculators** to see who owned which land and where to go to buy it. Within ten years of the Dawes Commission, the majority of Muscogee lands passed into the hands of settlers and oil speculators.

After dismantling tribal lands, the U.S. government sought to dismantle the tribal governments. In 1906, the U.S. Congress passed a law meant to do away with Native Americans' tribal governments. Under the new laws, the Muscogee Nation could no longer elect its own chiefs, leaders, and representatives. The federal government appointed the Muscogee Nation's leaders, and the nation lost all powers of **self-governance**. When Congress passed the Indian Reorganization Act in 1934, allowing tribes to reorganize their tribal governments, the act applied to all states except Oklahoma.

Assimilation into the white-American culture had always been a threat to the Muscogee people and to Native Americans in general, but the poverty the people faced in Oklahoma and the loss of tribal lands made that threat even more severe. In the 1950s, the federal government came up with a plan to improve the economic circumstances of tribal people in Oklahoma through *relocation*. This plan meant that the government took Native people from their homes and sent them to cities all over the United States.

Few economic and educational opportunities were in Oklahoma, and the government thought that by sending American Indians to other places, they would be giving them opportunities for education, job training, and employment. Unlike the Trail of Tears, this new relocation was voluntary, and many people joined the program. Some people faired well, finding jobs and bettering their economic circumstances. These positive outcomes,

A Portrait of Tribal Membership Today

Today, many Native American tribes have a "blood quantum" requirement for membership in the tribe. To be a member of the Muscogee Nation, you need not have a certain percentage of Indian blood, but you must be able to trace your ancestry back to one of the tribal members who received land during the Dawes Commission. To run for public office, however, you must be at least a quarter Muscogee Indian. Of the 53,719 members of the Muscogee Nation:

- 1,553 are full-blooded Creek (meaning that they only have Creek ancestors—none of their ancestors are from other cultures or other tribes).
- 3,994 members of the Muscogee Nation are one half Creek.
- 6,272 members of the Muscogee Nation are one quarter Creek.
- 41,800 members of the tribe have less than one quarter Creek ancestry.

According to the most recent population counts, there are currently 53,719 registered members of the Muscogee Nation. The tribe estimates that there are approximately twenty thousand more Muscogee descendents nationwide who have not registered with the tribe. About thirty thousand of the registered tribal members live within the Creek Nation boundaries in Oklahoma. Twenty-two of the people who originally received land under the provisions of the Dawes Commission are still alive. All of them are over one hundred years old.

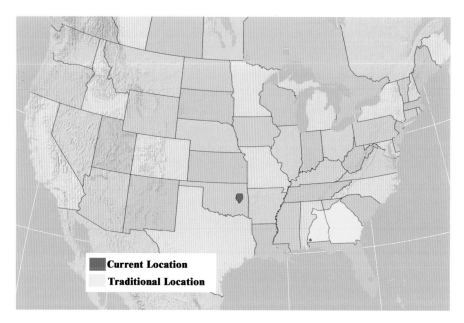

| Current Location |
| Traditional Location |

The Muscogee Confederacy once stretched across present-day Alabama and Georgia. The land owned by the Muscogee and Poarch Creek people today is only a fraction of what they held in the past.

however, did not always benefit the tribe, because many people who found success under relocation were assimilated into the American culture and lost their connection to the tribe and their traditions.

For other American Indians, the effects of relocation were personally devastating. The culture in American cities was very different from the culture they had been raised with in Oklahoma. In the Muscogee culture, individuals are members of large, extended families. In the American cities, many people felt lost, with no family or friends to support them. They also faced discrimination in the cities. Far from the support of their communities, many people did not know where to turn when wrongs were committed against them. Numerous individuals returned to Oklahoma disappointed with their experience and *disillusioned* with what America had to offer to them.

In the 1960s, some advances were made for the Muscogee Nation. For example, in 1964, the U.S. Supreme Court awarded four million dollars to the Muscogee Nation as *compensation* for land that was taken illegally.

However, not until 1970 was the Muscogee Nation once again allowed to elect its own chief.

The 1970s marked a turning point for the Muscogee Nation and for many Indian Nations. In 1971, Chief Claude Cox was freely elected by the Muscogee people, and in 1979, the nation *ratified* a new *constitution* that is still in use.

The last twenty years have been a time of great growth for the Muscogee Nation and for many other North American Indian tribes. Since being able to officially reorganize their tribal government, the Muscogee Nation has made huge strides in providing educational services, creating economic opportunities, improving health and health care, expanding tribal lands, preserving tribal history, and developing many other important projects. Now entering the twenty-first century, the Muscogee Nation is alive with many new hopes and goals.

> "There ought to be the strongest and most solemn assurance the country given them should be theirs as a permanent home for themselves and their posterity, without being disturbed by the encroachment of our cultures."
>
> —John C. Calhoun, Secretary of War under President Monroe

Continuing the Council Fire

The Muscogee people had been forced to start their towns and lives over with nothing but what they carried with them. One of the things they carried was fire. Back in the Southeast, the towns' fires had been very important symbols of unity, being carried from one town to another as the Muscogee Confederacy expanded. The fire represented the life of the town and its people. When the Muscogee people were removed to Indian Territory, each town carried live embers from its fire. As long as there were people to keep the fire burning, the town was still alive. In Indian Territory, the people reestablished their towns around these fires. For this reason, many of today's towns in Oklahoma have the same names as towns that once existed in Georgia and Alabama. Most of the original southeastern towns and fires of the Muscogee Confederacy were killed by the diseases and military campaigns of the Europeans, but forty-four of the original towns and fires came to Oklahoma, and seventeen of those forty-four are still burning today.

This council room at the Poarch Creek Indian headquarters is a place where government officials and community members can meet to discuss matters of importance for the tribe.

Chapter 3

The Poarch Band of Creek Indians: Yesterday and Today

Not all the Muscogee Indians were removed to Indian Territory in the Trail of Tears. When Andrew Jackson became president of the United States, a small number of those Indians who had supported Jackson in his military campaigns against Native people of the Southeast were rewarded with land grants in Alabama. The descendents of these original Muscogee Nation tribal members now make up the Poarch Creek Indian Tribe located in Escambia County, Alabama.

The fact that they had been guaranteed land did not make this group of Muscogee Indians safe from forced removal or from the theft of their land. At the beginning of the Trail of Tears, the U.S. Army was responsible for the removal of the Indians to the west, and they did not remove those people who had been granted land by Andrew Jackson. However, the U.S. government soon decided that they no longer wished to use the military for the removal, so they hired private **contractors** to finish the removal for

In Poarch, Alabama, many buildings proudly display the seal of the Poarch Creek Indians.

them. These men got paid by the person to round up the Native Americans and force them into Indian Territory. Since the contractors were paid for each person they were able to kidnap and transport, they did not care if certain people were supposed to be permitted to remain in the Southeast, so many of the Lower Creeks who had been promised land and protection were eventually forcibly removed to Indian Territory as well.

As the Muscogee Nation in Oklahoma was being ripped apart by the Civil War, the Creek people left in Alabama were also suffering. The Civil War was a horrific time for the entire nation of America, but conditions were especially hard for those in the South. The North, with its many industries, was always the wealthier part of the nation. Much of the South's wealth was based on agriculture (most of it conducted using slave labor). With the outbreak of the Civil War, the South was cut off, not only from the North's wealth, but also from the different goods the North manufactured and supplied. To make matters worse, with all the men fighting in the war, not enough people were left to run even small family farms, let alone the huge plantations that were the greatest source of wealth for the South. In these *dire* economic conditions, many people had to sell their possessions, lost their land, and even starved to death. Then, when Northern soldiers marched into the South, they destroyed many crops, homes, and cities. Many historical records were lost, including records about the Creek people in the South. Today, in European countries such as England and France, you can find information about the South and the Creek Indians that you cannot find in the United States. This is because those records in the United States were destroyed in the *conflagration* of the war, but the records housed in Europe remained safe.

Even after the Civil War, the Creek people left in Alabama faced numerous difficulties. In 1924, *patents* were issued for land in Alabama. Without the benefit of a tribal government to fight for the tribal members as a group, and without the money or ability to hire lawyers to represent their claims individually, much of the Creeks' land that had been granted to them by Jackson was lost.

For many decades, the Indians of Poarch, Alabama, worked to settle their land claims and improve educational and economic opportunities for their people. But again, without a federally recognized tribal government to petition and deal with the U.S. government, it was difficult for the individual people of the community to get their grievances acknowledged and addressed.

Just because the federal government did not recognize the Poarch Creek Indians as a tribe, however, did not mean that they did not see themselves as a tribe. The Poarch Creek Indians were still a tribal community, united

Part of a Community

Despite receiving recognition as an Indian tribe in 1984, the Poarch Creek Indians do not try to isolate themselves from their non-Indian neighbors. The Poarch Creek tribe places a huge emphasis on being part of the larger community. As Community Relations Director Roy Shivers explains, it is important to the tribe that it creates economic, educational, and cultural opportunities not just for tribal members but for all people in the Atmore community and beyond.

under tribal leaders, and concerned about common goals. Calvin W. McGhee was an important leader of the Poarch Tribe in the early and middle part of the twentieth century. He worked to settle land claims and pushed for the federal government to officially recognize the Poarch people as a tribe with a *legitimate* tribal government.

The year 1984 was a *watershed* year for the Poarch Creek Indians. In 1984, the *Bureau of Indian Affairs* finally recognized the Poarch Creek Indians as an Indian tribe. In 1985, 229.54 acres (almost 93 hectares) of land were taken into trust as a reservation for the Poarch tribe. The Poarch Band of Creek Indians is now the only federally recognized tribe in the state of Alabama.

Recognition of the tribe by the federal and state governments has opened

These stones lie in the Judson Indian Cemetery, one of four cemeteries currently being restored by the Poarch Creek Tribe.

Many things changed for the Poarch Creek people when the federal government finally recognized them as an Indian tribe. Their newly recognized tribal government focused on economic expansion, allowing them to build government and community buildings like this complex that currently houses offices, conference rooms, and a health center.

many doors for the Poarch people. Since 1984, some of the main projects of the Poarch tribe have included developing a tribal government and court system, building affordable housing for tribal members, increasing educational and economic opportunities, finding new ways to preserve and re-discover tribal culture and history, and increasing the tribe's land holdings.

Today, the Poarch Creek Tribe has 460 acres (186 hectares) of reservation land as well as sixteen hundred additional acres (648 hectares) of purchased land. Currently, approximately twenty-five hundred registered members make up the Poarch Creek tribe. About fifteen hundred of these members live within thirty miles (48.2 kilometers) of the Poarch Creek Reservation. Members of the Poarch tribe see themselves not only as members of the Poarch Creek community but also as members of the larger community of southern Alabama. The Poarch tribe is currently the largest employer (for both Native and non-Native people) in the area, one of the largest providers of social and community services and activities, and one of the most important financial supporters and political **lobbyists** for the area's public schools.

The seal of the Supreme Court of the Muscogee Nation of Oklahoma graces this door of the judicial offices. The seal depicts warriors playing the sacred stickball game.

Chapter 4

Government and Justice Systems: Past and Present

When the Muscogee people lived in the Southeast, their government was based on the tribal towns and tribal clans. Each town and clan of the Muscogee Confederacy was considered either White or Red. All towns had members of both Red and White clans, but if the majority of the clans were Red, then the town was considered a Red town. If the majority of clans represented in the town were White, then the town would be a White town. The White towns were in charge of peaceful matters, while the Red towns were in charge of the responsibilities of war. Red towns and White towns often formed athletic rivalries. They would play each other in stick-ball tournaments, a game that was very important to Muscogee life and culture.

Each tribal town had a *micco*, or **civil** chief, who was responsible for management of **communal** food stores, speaking with **ambassadors** of other towns, tribes, and groups, negotiating treaties and peace agreements, and

The Creek Council House in Okmulgee, Oklahoma, once held historic meetings of its House of Kings and House of Warriors and stood as a symbol of peace, unity, and determination for the native people living in Indian Territory. Today this building and what it stood for live on as the Creek Council House Museum.

overseeing ceremonial and hunt celebrations. However, all of these individual duties fell under the largest duty of maintaining harmony within the talwa. To do this, the micco had to be a **diplomatic** person who could listen to all sides of an issue and successfully **negotiate** settlements that would be acceptable to everyone concerned. If a micco could not fulfill these duties and achieve harmony, he was removed and a new one chosen.

Another responsibility of the micco was to choose his governing council. Tribal towns had three types of government advisors. The first was the *tvstvnvke*, or war chief. The micco chose the tvstvnvke from the Red Clan members of the town. The tvstvnvke was in charge of maintaining public order, organizing stickball games with other towns, advising the micco on matters relating to war, and if a war were to break out, organizing the warriors and leading them to battle.

The micco's second tier of advisors was the *henneha*. The henneha advised the micco on public works projects. They oversaw the labor in the communal fields where the food for the community was grown, they organized the building of new homes for tribal members, and they prepared an important ceremonial drink called "black drink" for the weekly council meetings. After each meeting, the Speaker (one of the henneha who was chosen as the micco's spokesperson) would relay the micco's decisions to the members of the town.

The final group of advisors was the *este vcakvike*, meaning "beloved old men." The este vcakvike were elders who were known in the tribe for dis-

In Okmulgee, Oklahoma, members of the Muscogee Nation can gather in this assembly hall to voice their opinions and concerns on tribal matters.

playing wisdom throughout their lives. These men were greatly honored and carefully chosen to convey their many years of wisdom in the form of good advice to the micco.

The Muscogee form of government was a democratic one in which every member's point of view was considered important. The government's ultimate goal was to make sure that every issue was decided to the satisfaction of every group concerned. This is different from a majority rule system in which, for example, everyone might vote for a person or policy, but then the majority wins and the minority is left unrepresented or unsatisfied.

Matters of crime and punishment were usually handled within each individual clan. For any justice system to be successful, the justice system must have clear goals. The justice system of the Muscogee people had two main goals: to mend the broken law by righting the wrong that had been committed and to cleanse the **perpetrator** of the crime, making him innocent again.

Counseling clan members and deciding punishments for **indiscretions** were the responsibilities of the eldest male in the clan. In cases where a

---

More Than a Game

The game of stickball was an important part of Muscogee life. It was not merely a game of enjoyment and skill, but was also a means of settling serious debates. If two parties could not reconcile a difference of opinion or conflict, they would sometimes play a game of stickball. The winner of the game was then the victor of the argument and granted decision-making power. Sometimes, a game of stickball would even be played as a battle in war. By battling with a ball and stick, rather than weapons, a clear victor could be determined without any loss of life. This might seem like a strange way to fight a war, but even people who are at war hope to someday have peace. Think how much easier it would be to make peace after battle if no one was killed in the war!

person of one clan committed a crime against a member of another clan, and if the two clans could not reach their own agreement about punishment, the tribal council would be asked to settle the dispute.

The most serious crime a person could commit was to kill another person. It did not matter if the killing were accidental or purposeful; the crime still had to be punished. However, the killer might be punished in different ways. On the one hand, the family of the killer's victim might decide that the killer deserved the death penalty. On the other hand, sometimes the family of the victim would adopt the killer, having the killer take the deceased person's place. A large part of the harm done by the killer was to leave the victim's family with one less person to contribute to supporting the family. Therefore, the killer could help ease the family's loss by performing the duties of the deceased person.

When the Civil War was over, the Muscogee people struggled to reunite their nation. In an effort to heal from the divisions created within the tribe, the Muscogee Nation adopted a constitution in 1867. The tribe had never before had one document declaring the governmental system and laws for the whole nation. The nation built a large, log council house in which resided the *legislative* bodies of the new government, the House of Warriors and the House of Kings. The House of Warriors was made up of warriors who served as representatives of the people; the House of Kings was made up of the chiefs. In this council house, the Muscogee Nation had historic gatherings, not just of their own chiefs and leaders, but of leaders from all the tribes in Indian Territory. When the original council house

The Light Horsemen (the police officers of the Muscogee Nation) serve not only as tribal police officers but as officers of the county as well.

burned in 1878, a stone building was erected in its place, four times the size of the original meeting place. The new council house stood as a symbol of progress and unity for the Muscogee people and the tribes of Oklahoma.

In 1906 through 1907, when tribal governments were disbanded and Oklahoma became a state, the Department of the Interior took control of the council house. The town of Okmulgee, where the council house stands, later purchased the building. Though the building has never been returned to the tribe, it is now the Creek Council House Museum and a home to much of the history of the Muscogee Nation in Oklahoma.

In 1979, the Muscogee Nation ratified a new constitution and reorganized its governments. Today, the government of the Muscogee Nation of Oklahoma consists of numerous offices and departments. A chief and second chief serve similar roles to those of the president and vice president in the U.S. government. The chief and second chief are each elected for a four-year term and can serve up to two terms.

The tribe also has a national council with a speaker, second speaker, national council secretary, and legislative research specialist. Each of the political districts in the Muscogee Nation has representatives. The Muscogee Nation's national council and district representatives could be thought of as similar to the United States's Senate and House of Representatives.

Like the U.S. government, the Muscogee Nation's government also has a judicial branch in the form of a supreme court. The Muscogee Nation is self-governing, which includes creating and enforcing its own laws. In most cases, crimes committed by members of the Muscogee Nation within Muscogee Nation boundaries are dealt with, prosecuted, and resolved within the tribe. The tribe has its own tribal police force, called the Light Horsemen. The Light Horsemen are cross-deputized, meaning that they serve both as tribal police for the Muscogee Nation and as county police for the larger community. Cases that are not resolved in the lower Muscogee courts are brought to the *Este Cvte Mvskoke Etvlwv Fvtceckv Cuko Hvlwat*, the Muscogee Nation's supreme court. Decisions made by the Muscogee courts are considered legally binding by the state of Oklahoma and can only be overruled by federal courts if they somehow infringe on federal laws.

When the Poarch Creek were recognized as a tribe in 1986, they also had to form a tribal government. Like the U.S. government and the Muscogee Nation, the government formed by the Poarch Creek tribe has a legislative,

---

A Message to Young People

Second Chief A. D. Ellis has been serving the Muscogee community for many years, both as a National Council member and as the second chief. Mr. Ellis was a farmer, a member of the military, and the owner of a small trucking company before entering public service. He would like to encourage more young people to think about someday serving the tribe as council members and chiefs. He says of his own experience: "I thought I was living a good life until I got into office. The feeling you get from helping people is the greatest feeling in the world."

executive, and judicial branch. The legislative branch consists of nine elected council members and a tribal administrator, or chairperson. The position of tribal administrator is similar to the position of chief in the Muscogee Nation or the position of president of the United States. In the Poarch Creek Tribe, Eddie Tullis has served in the position of tribal administrator for twenty-five years (he was already serving in this position before recognition of the tribe by the federal government) and has seen many positive changes for the tribe in that time.

The executive branch of the Poarch Creek tribe has many different departments that oversee the daily activities and needs of the tribe:

- central administration
- accounting
- employment and training
- education
- social services
- health services
- community services
- public safety
- public works
- tribal enrollment

- environmental protection
- economic development
- tribal utilities
- tribal court and planning
- real estate

The judicial branch of the government consists of a tribal court system as well as a law enforcement staff. The tribal police officers are cross-deputized, so they serve both the Poarch Creek community and the larger community of Escambia County. Crimes committed within the reservation are prosecuted within the tribal court system. The Alabama State court system has no authority to prosecute crimes committed on the reservation, and the federal court system only has authority in major criminal cases.

Second Chief A.D. Ellis works hard to serve his nation and hopes that Muscogee youth will follow in his footsteps.

The Poarch Creek Tribe's fire department is the first responder to emergencies in the Atmore, Alabama, area. The fire departments of the Poarch Creek and Muscogee Nation provide important services, not just to their own tribal communities, but to the surrounding communities as well.

When the Poarch Creek Indians became a federally recognized tribe, they drafted a set of goals for their new tribal government. They state their goals as follows:

- Continue forever, with the help of God our Creator, our unique identity as members of the Poarch Band of Creek Indians, and to protect that identity from forces that threaten to diminish it;
- Protect our inherent rights as members of a sovereign American Indian tribe;
- Promote our cultural and religious beliefs and to pass them in our own way to our children, grandchildren and grandchildren's children forever;
- Help our members achieve their highest potential in education, physical and mental health and economic development;

- Maintain good relations with other Indian tribes, the United States, the State of Alabama, and local governments;
- Support the government of the United States and encourage our members to be loyal citizens;
- Acquire, develop, and conserve resources to achieve economic and social self-sufficiency for our tribe;
- Ensure that our people shall live in peace and harmony among ourselves and with all other people.

Both the Poarch Creek Indians and the Muscogee Nation seek to govern their people with justice. Their government structure may be patterned after American models—but their values are still rooted deep in their cultural heritage.

Respect and Punishment

Even when dealing out punishment, the Muscogee people always treated individual life with great respect. For example, in Muscogee society, people were not imprisoned. Punishments were quickly decided and carried out so that the offender could become an innocent and productive member of society again. If a person was given the death sentence, he was released to spend time with his family and get his affairs in order. This time before execution was usually about five months, which allowed the person to help his family harvest the current season's crops or plant for the next year. This way, the person could be assured that his family would be prepared and properly cared for once he was gone. At the end of this time, two things ensured that a person would show up for his punishment. The first was honor. Personal and family honor was highly valued in Muscogee society. To dishonor one's self or family was so abhorrent to the Muscogee people that they generally preferred accepting punishment to being dishonored. The other assurance that a person would accept his punishment was that, if he did not, a member of his family would have to accept the punishment in his place.

A young Creek man dances in elaborate dress in Poarch, Alabama. (His costume is not, however, typical of the Muscogee people of Oklahoma.) Dancing has traditionally been both a social and sacred event, but the dancing featured here is part of the modern powwow movement.

Chapter 5

Economic Opportunities and Social Services

The Muscogee Nation is one of the largest employers and social service providers in the area. The tribe currently employs fifteen hundred people, of which fourteen hundred are Native American. People are employed in numerous positions, from jobs as assistants, secretaries, and administrators in the tribal headquarters, to positions in research and historic preservation, to jobs in the tribal police department and the tribal newspaper. The tribe's casinos and service plazas currently employ four hundred people.

The largest portion of tribal funds comes from taxes. Since the Muscogee Nation is an independent government, it is free to set and collect its own taxes. The most profitable taxes for the tribe are the fuel and cigarette taxes. The second largest source of funds is "Indian gaming," a name given to the explosion of bingo halls and casinos on tribal lands.

In some ways, casinos and bingo halls are very controversial. The controversy tends to come from state officials and religious organizations that believe gambling is wrong or that it will attract crime. Within the Indian communities, however, people have seen how gaming has saved the tribes from desperate financial circumstances, allowing them to become more independent and to no longer rely entirely on the federal government for financial support. Native Americans have seen time and time again that the American government cannot always be relied on to adequately address a tribe's needs, so every opportunity for independence is seized with enthusiasm. The Muscogee Nation feels that only through economic independence can they gain true political independence. Indian gaming is an important opportunity for independence.

Despite the fact that gaming has been extremely profitable, not everyone sees it as a long-term solution to the Muscogee Nation's economic concerns. Second Chief Ellis, for example, acknowledges the positive effects of gaming, both in revenue and in job creation for the tribe. However, he would like to see the tribe extend its economic ventures beyond gaming. The four hundred jobs within the casinos are a good step, he says, but those jobs have no room for growth, advancement, or promotion. One day,

This center provides a place for community members to socialize and receive services.

The Creek Bingo Palace has been an important source of income for the Poarch Creek Tribe. The money bingo brings in allows the tribe to be more self-sufficient and offer much-needed services to the community.

Mr. Ellis would like to see companies and industries that give the people more chance for education, promotion, and advancement. He would also like to see the tribe develop a job creation program for people who have little education and are on welfare.

Another important focus for the Muscogee Tribe is social services. The most important concerns in this area are health and housing. In the tribe's current health system, those who have private insurance use that insurance instead of relying on tribal funds for health care. Those without private insurance, however, have their health care costs covered by the tribe. With thirty thousand tribal members living within the tribal service area, adequate funding for health care is a constant problem.

Funding for housing is also an immediate concern. The Muscogee Na-

Creek Indian Enterprises oversees economic development and management of Poarch Creek tribal businesses.

tion began a housing program in 1969 to make high-quality, affordable housing available to eligible tribal members. Since the program began, the tribe has built 1,900 homes and is currently building new homes at a rate of fifty per year. Tribal members who have a home built through this program pay fifty to one hundred dollars per month, with payments increasing as the person's income increases. The homeowner has twenty-five interest-free years in which to pay for their home. The tribe has also built 360 low-rent apartments. In addition to these programs, the tribe *rehabilitates* private homes and has a program in which the Muscogee Nation pays the down payment and closing costs for homes that tribal members wish to purchase. Currently, all money for housing programs comes from the federal government. Lack of funds makes it difficult to fill the need for housing. Currently, 740 people are on the waiting list for houses, and some have been on the list for ten years.

While federal money goes toward housing, most tribal money goes toward education. The Muscogee Nation runs a childcare facility to care for the children of working parents; it also has a federally *subsidized Head*

Start Program. The Johnson O'Malley Program gives money to schools for things such as playground equipment and sports programs, while the Muscogee Nation works to improve the public schools in general for all students by providing services such as before- and after-school programs. The tribe also works with the state to make sure the public schools address the specific needs of Native students by including Native issues in class-room *curriculum*. In addition to these educational programs, rehabilitation programs help youth with issues concerning substance abuse and crime.

While the Muscogee Nation strives to provide opportunities to its youth, it also provides many services to its senior citizens. The tribe has elder nu-trition programs as well as a senior citizen center where seniors gather daily for lunch, activities, and socializing. There is also a gift shop that sells crafts the senior citizens make to fund their annual trips.

The Poarch Creek tribe is also working hard for its people. Employing 160 people in its administration and 350 people in its industries, the Poarch Creek tribe is one of the largest employers in Escambia County. In an effort to create economic growth and opportunity, the tribal council formed Creek Indian Enterprises (CIE) in 1988. A five-member board of directors

What Does a Fish Farmer Do All Day?

Aquaculture is a type of agriculture, except the crop is grown in the water instead of on land. Aquaculture is the farming of fish and shellfish. What makes aquaculture different from regular fishing is that the animals are not taken from the wild. They are raised in controlled environments, like artificial ponds built specifically for the purpose of raising these animals for food. Instead of planting crops, milking cows, or working the fields all day, a fish-farmer must feed his "stocks" and pay attention to water quality, making sure that his ponds have enough oxygen, stay at a healthy temperature for the fish, and are free of pollutants. Some of the most commonly farmed fish are catfish and salmon, but crawfish and shrimp farming are also big industries. Because our oceans and waterways are so over fished, much of the fish sold in restaurants and grocery stores today comes from farms.

runs Creek Indian Enterprises with the purpose of developing and managing economic ventures for the tribe.

As happened with many other tribes, the Poarch Creek tribe has found gaming to be an extremely profitable business. The Poarch Creek tribe began its gaming operations in a complex housing the Creek Bingo Palace, the Creek Smoke Shop, and Palace Printing. With the success of this complex, the tribe has opened other gaming facilities in additional locations. About one mile (1.6 kilometers) from the Creek Bingo Palace is the Best Western of Atmore and the Creek Family Restaurant, also profitable tribal businesses.

In addition to the gaming business, the Poarch Creek tribe operates Per-

Eddie Tullis has served as chief of the Poarch Creek Tribe for more than twenty-five years. The tribe has made many advancements in economic and social services under his leadership.

A herd of sheep grazes on Poarch Creek lands. They are one of the agricultural projects overseen by Perdido River Farms, a Creek Indian Enterprise.

dido River Farms, a large agricultural project that extends over approximately 1,160 acres (470 hectares) of tribally owned land. On this land, crops such as soybeans, cotton, wheat, and corn are grown, and land is leased to area farmers. Cattle and sheep graze in pastures. The farm is also home to an aquaculture business; twelve acres (approximately 5 hectares) of the farm hold catfish ponds in which catfish are raised for sale. The farm also has 178 beautiful acres (72 hectares) of pecan trees.

One of the most exciting Poarch Creek business projects is the joining and expanding of Muskogee Metalworks and Manufacturing Technology, Inc. Muskogee Metalworks manufactures various types of metal parts for military and commercial uses. Manufacturing Technology, Inc. designs and manufactures high-tech military electronics, hardware, and software. The Poarch Creek tribe recently purchased and opened a new facility where they can combine these two businesses and dramatically increase their size, number of employees, and work capacity. Muskogee Metalworks and Manufacturing Technology, Inc. received a multi-million dollar contract

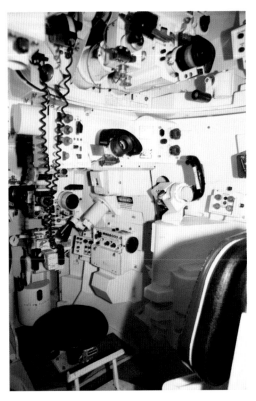

This tank simulator, produced by Muskogee Metal Works and Manufacturing Technology, Inc., will help train soldiers to use military equipment.

with the U.S. Department of Defense. Currently, they are building metal parts for missiles and tank simulators in which soldiers train for battle.

In addition to economic opportunities, the Poarch Creek tribe also offers many social and community services. One of the most impressive projects the tribe has developed is its housing project. When you arrive at the administration complex of the Poarch Creek tribe, you see a small neighborhood of homes. At first, it might look like any other neighborhood, but if you look closer, you may be surprised by how well kept and pristine each home looks. Each housing unit has its own spacious yard and paved driveway. Many have carefully planted flowerbeds, gardens, and trees. Some have yellow ribbons showing support for family members in the military and troops abroad. Many fly the American flag. This is the senior citizen community built and managed by the Poarch Creek Indian Housing Authority.

These buildings are rented at a low cost to seniors and individuals with special needs, such as physical disabilities. Despite the fact that the individuals living in these houses do not actually own the homes, one of the most impressive things about the community is the sense of independence and individual ownership the neighborhood conveys. Roy Shivers comments that it is important that the members of this neighborhood feel a sense of pride, ownership, and independence in their homes. The neighborhood is located next to the health clinic, so the seniors have easy access to any medical services they may require. A nurse visits people in

Roy Shivers is the Community Relations Director of the Poarch Creek Tribe. Much of his job focuses on the tribe's relationship with the surrounding Atmore, Alabama, community.

The Truth About Taxes

One of the most common misconceptions non-Native people have about American Indians is that they do not have to pay taxes. This is false. In fact, some Native people end up paying more taxes than do non-Native people. In the Muscogee Nation, citizens must pay tribal taxes, state taxes, and federal taxes.

their homes, and tribal vans drive the senior citizens to the health center as well as to the senior citizen center, where people like to meet for lunch, activities, and socialization.

The Housing Authority also has four other low-rent subdivisions. These subdivisions offer two- and three-bedroom homes to tribal members for

The greased pig chase is a favorite event at the Poarch Creek Thanksgiving Pow Wow. The catching of the greased pig provides great entertainment for the crowd and lots of exercise for the participating youngsters!

A Poarch Creek softball team gears up for a game. The Poarch Creek Indian tribe's softball teams play an important role in this southern Alabama community. Both native and non-native children play on the tribe's teams.

rents of one hundred to one hundred fifty dollars per month. In addition, if tribal members wish to build a new house, the tribe will build and finance the house. The new homeowner will have thirty years to pay the tribe back without interest.

The Indian Health Program is another impressive accomplishment of the Poarch Creek Community. A **comprehensive** clinic offers medical, dental, community health, and pharmacy services. These services are free to tribal members. If a tribal member needs a service, such as a serious operation, that the clinic cannot provide, the tribe will pay for the person's medical care at another facility.

The Poarch Volunteer Fire Department plays another important role in the surrounding community and is a great source of pride for the tribe. The

Horseshoes is a popular event in the Senior Olympics held by the Poarch Creek Indian Tribe each year.

fire department is the largest volunteer department in the area and the first respondent for any accident occurring within a seventeen-mile (29-kilometer) area. In addition to its protective duties, the fire department also plays a huge role in community building through responsibilities such as writing and producing the *Poarch Creek News* (the tribe's monthly newsletter) and coordinating the Annual Poarch Creek Indian Thanksgiving Pow Wow, a two-day event that the whole Poarch community plans and accomplishes together. The **powwow** draws between ten and twenty thousand visitors to the tribe each year.

The Annual Poarch Creek Indian Thanksgiving Pow Wow is an excellent example of how the Poarch Creek tribe brings opportunity, growth, and prosperity to its own tribal members as well as to the entire community.

The thousands of people who attend this event every year enjoy the special honor of experiencing and participating in Native American culture. Visitors watch competitive dancing featuring dancers from tribes all over North and South America, see the traditional and contemporary work of Native artists, and enjoy delicious Native foods like roasted corn (a secret recipe that no one outside of Poarch is going to get their hands on!). Members of the tribe benefit from the powwow financially and through the opportunity it provides for people to express their culture and reestablish their traditions. Many children in the Native community today have been raised without their traditional culture, and events like powwows allow these children to learn about and reconnect with the traditions before they are forgotten. The community and businesses of Atmore also benefit from the powwow by sharing in their neighbor's traditions and by the business that the thousands of visitors bring. If you are looking for a different way to celebrate Thanksgiving this year, you should think about making a trip to southern Alabama!

According to Creek tradition, when the earliest People first emerged from the fog, they grasped each other in love. Twenty-first-century Creek may express their sense of commitment to each other in very different ways from those long-ago People. Each in their own way, however, the Poarch Creek tribe and the Muscogee Nation are both caring for their members. They are looking for ways to improve the lives of each Creek, and they are ensuring that their people have opportunities to grow and prosper.

The land was formed between the water and the sky.

Chapter 6

Spirituality

First there was only water and air. New animals were coming, though, and they would need land on which to live. So the crawfish went down below to see about new land. He carried what he found back to the Council Fire.

The animals gathered around the Council Fire grew silent to hear what crawfish had learned about the new lands. He said the new land was a good place where fish could swim, birds could live, and where animals could walk and find food. "Here," he said, "I have the new land in my claws. Look how good it will be to live upon."

The mighty eagle looked at what the crawfish held in his claws and stepped to the center to speak. "We have great joy in our hearts because of these new lands, but we must prepare them for the coming of the animals. Will the council give me permission to help create the better land below?"

"Yes, Mighty Eagle," the council cried, "Help us to make this land below a good place to live."

So Eagle took the mud and sand from Crawfish's claws and rolled it into a ball. Holding the ball in his strong legs, he spread his powerful wings. The Council felt a great wind rush over them as Eagle soared into the air high above their heads. Up and up he went, flapping his mighty wings until he was flying higher than any bird had flown before.

Dana Tiger's painting Our Tradition *depicts women dancing. Dancing has always been an important part of Muscogee spiritual life.*

The Council looked up. Eagle was just a small speck in the sky, and they wondered where he was going with the land Crawfish had carried from down below. Perhaps he was going to fly away with the land. Perhaps he was stealing it, they thought.

But then, when the Eagle was as high as he could go, he threw the red ball of earth down as hard as he could. The ball blazed like a roaring shooting star past the Council. It hit the waters so hard that it separated the vast ocean into two and sent a huge wave out across the waters. The soil hit the water with such force that the ball flattened out into one vast land called the Earth. This new land was very wet, so Eagle spread his wings again and flew over the Earth. The flapping of his wings created a great wind that made the Earth dry. Then the animal migration began.

This is how the Earth was formed between the water and the sky.

Stories are the foundations for understanding who we are; they are an important part of all peoples and cultures. Wherever you go in life, you will

This young boy in Poarch, Alabama, is already participating in dancing at a young age.

The stomp dance is performed in many different tribes. These ceremonial grounds belong to the Cherokee, but typical Creek stomp grounds will also have a central fire surrounded by four arbors.

find stories. The stories we tell each other may sometimes seem like entertainment, but they are a vital part of our existence. Stories are spiritual things, for they teach us about where we came from, why we are here, and how we should live in the world.

For the Muscogee people, stories have always been an important part of life and spirituality. For people like the long-ago Muscogee who had no written language, storytelling was especially important. It was through storytelling that the history of the people was kept alive and passed on through the generations of the tribe. The storyteller was a historian, teacher, and an entertainer, a very important person in the tribe. A future storyteller was selected (usually from the boys of the tribe) at a young age and spent his youth with the storyteller, learning the tribe's history and training in the art of storytelling. Storytellers were so important to the tribe that they were usually not permitted into battle, for the storyteller might be killed and all his knowledge and the tribe's history lost. When the storyteller died, the young man he had trained became the new storyteller and took an *apprentice* of his own. In this way, the stories of the Muscogee people have been passed on since the Beginning.

Stories are often about beginnings. Every Native American tribe has a *creation story*, which tells how the tribe began and how the earth, animals, and plants were created. Many tribes also have stories about each other, which tell the people of one tribe how other people came to be.

When Europeans came to North America, they were a great mystery to the people already living there, for the Native people had no stories about these light-skinned newcomers. Without *origin* stories, they did not understand who these people were, where they came from, or what their purpose was for coming to the land. These "storyless" people also brought plants and animals with them that the Native people had never seen. To give meaning to these new people, plants, and animals, many new stories developed in the Native tribes. These stories were meant to give these new things history and meaning. One very interesting story in the Muscogee culture tells how the Muscogee people accepted European descendants and foods into the culture.

When the Others came to the land, they made homes for themselves and began to grow crops. The Others made the People believe that they were coming in peace, so the People treated the Others peacefully and lived with them as neighbors and then as friends.

Some of the Others and the People fell in love. Love is as old as time, so some of the People took Others as wives and had children with them.

Respecting Ceremonial Grounds

When you enter the Poarch Creek Ceremonial Grounds, you pass a sign that reads: "Do not take photographs. This is our Church. Please respect it." Many non-Native people think they have a right to visit Native people's ceremonial grounds, watch the ceremonies, take pictures of what they see, and even participate in the dances. This is very hurtful to many Native people who feel that their sacred way of life is treated like a tourist attraction by such visitors. Many people forget that being permitted to see a person's private spiritual life is an incredible *privilege* and great honor and should always be treated with the *utmost* respect and appreciation.

Then there was a new problem for the tribe, for the Other women had no clan, and therefore their children had no clan. It is a bad thing to be without a clan. Without a clan, you have no family, no brothers and sisters, no mothers and fathers, no place where you belong. You must never marry members of your own clan, but these children had no clan, so how would they find husbands and wives? It was a big problem for the People and for the children who were not fully accepted as members of the tribe.

The mothers of the clanless ones were very sad for their children whom they loved, so they went to the Elders to ask what could be done. The Elders told the women that they must take a journey together to pray to the Creator. The Creator would be able to see their hearts and know if their hearts were pure. Then, if they were pure of heart, the Creator would hear their prayers.

The Tallahassee Methodist Church is one of the churches where members of the Muscogee Nation of Oklahoma worship.

The women knew that what the Elders said was true, so they went out from the village and prayed to the Creator. They were humble and filled with longing as they sent their prayers from their troubled hearts. They stayed there for many days, praying in this way, and the Creator saw that their hearts were pure.

The Creator told the women to journey out from the village to the place where the land becomes soft and the waters turn black. He told them to stay in this place until they found a plant that cried out to them from beneath the ground. It was from this plant, the Creator said, that their children would receive a clan name. But the plant would do even more than give the children a name. It would also be a gift to feed the People forever.

Trusting in the Creator, the women set out for the place of soft ground and black water. It was a place filled with frightening things. Insects crawled upon their skin, and snakes wrapped themselves about the women's ankles. Thorns stuck in their feet and hungry logs and strange spirits surrounded them. Together the women moved through the land. Holding the love of their children and husbands in their hearts, believing in the Creator's instructions, they searched bravely for the root that would cry out to them.

They stayed in this place among the spiders and the waters for many days. Hope began to fade in their hearts, but the women would not give up their search. Instead of despairing, they cried out to the Creator again, and when they did so, they heard a voice calling out to them from beneath the ground.

The women dug where they heard the plant. When the plant was dug up it spoke to them. "Even though I am from below the ground," it said, "the Creator has given me eyes to see in all directions at the same time. Take me to the village and cut out my eyes. Plant my eyes in a mound and I promise to feed the People forever."

The women cut out the plant's eyes and planted them in a mound. When they did this, their children became the White Potato Clan, and the plant continues to feed the people to this day.

Stories, of course, are not the only way in which spirituality is celebrated or expressed. Ceremony is an important part of all religious life, and like their stories, Muscogee ceremonies have been passed down through all generations.

The most important ceremony of the Muscogee people is still the Green Corn Ceremony. This ceremony happens once a year, when the first corn becomes ripe. The Green Corn Ceremony is a time of healing and renewal for the Muscogee people. A traditional Green Corn Ceremony was conducted in the following way.

Preparations for the ceremony would begin well in advance with women making new clothing and pottery for their families, cleaning out their homes, and throwing away things that had become broken and useless during the year. The men prepared the ceremonial grounds and buildings and brought four large logs into the square. The logs were placed with the ends facing toward each other, making a shape like a cross. Each log pointed out in one of the four directions, representing the north, east, south, and west.

On the first day, all the people would gather in the ceremonial grounds of the town. By rubbing two sticks together, the men would light a fire at the place where the four logs met. This starting of the fire symbolized the rekindling of the tribe. In the evening, a ceremonial stickball game would be played.

The most important event on the second day of the ceremony was usually the women's dance. All dances had deep meanings about life in the tribe and the relationships between people and the natural world. In the evening, another game of stickball might be played.

On the third day of the ceremony, the men would fast and drink the "black drink," which made them vomit. This was a time to cleanse their bodies. Then the men would hold a tribal court in which all crimes were acknowledged and forgiven. This was also a time to renew marriages, become divorced, or emerge from widowhood. At the end of the third day, the tribe was considered clean from wrongdoings of the past. The men would bathe and dance four times. Then everyone would join in the dancing. The fire would burn and the dancing continue until the dawn of the fourth day. Sometimes the Green Corn Ceremony would continue for more than four days, but the ceremony always ended with a feast day in which the whole tribe would partake in the new green corn.

Today, though many things have changed for the Muscogee people, and the Green Corn Ceremony may not always be celebrated the way it was in the past, it is still a ceremony of great importance for those who maintain traditional beliefs.

If you drive back on a long, red road through the forest of southern Alabama, you will come to the sacred stomp dance grounds. Every Saturday afternoon, *traditionalist* families gather here to renew their ties to each other and celebrate their lives and culture. Members of the Poarch Creek tribe gather weekly to perform the ceremony of the stomp dance. The grounds are located in a beautiful, secluded spot in the forest. In this place, there is a small hill that rises within a circle of trees. On the top of the hill are four brush **arbors** built in the traditional way. In the middle of the arbors is the fire and the stomp dance ground. One arbor stands to the north of the fire, one to the east, one to the south, and one to the west. Traditionally, visitors from tribes to the north stood in the north arbor. Visitors from the east stood in the east arbor, and so on around the fire. A circle of ground is worn bare from the many feet that have passed over it in celebration. Each Saturday, when the sun begins to set, the stomp dancers begin dancing in a circle around the fire. They dance throughout the night until the sun rises the next morning.

Though people gather weekly to celebrate the stomp dance, traditionalists are actually in the minority in the Poarch Creek tribe. Today, most people practice Christian beliefs and are members of such churches as the Baptist and Methodist. Missionaries from many different Christian religions were often some of the first people to make contact with the Native people of North America. Many contemporary members of the Poarch Creek tribe and Muscogee Nation are devout Christians.

On the one hand, missionaries were some of the first people to bring diseases to many tribes and often opened the door to the use of military forces against Native people. When Native people resisted the missionaries and tried to drive them away from the tribe, military units were often brought in to protect the missions.

On the other hand, however, missionary work also had positive effects. Missions often provided educational opportunities to tribal members when no other such opportunities existed. Missions also brought economic and medical aid to the people. Many elements of Christian beliefs are compatible with traditional Native spiritual beliefs. This is one of the reasons that Christianity became so popular among the Native people of North America. If the basic principles of the religion were completely foreign or contradictory to traditional beliefs, there would have been a greater resistance to Christianity. Joyce Bear, the Historic Preservation Officer of the Muscogee Nation in Oklahoma estimates that today about one third of the Muscogee people are Christians, one third are traditionalists, and one third of the population practices a mixture of the two belief systems.

Celebration of Determination *by Dana Tiger*.

Chapter 7

Contributions

Do you think *democratic* government is an idea that the European settlers in America came up with? It's not. The idea of democratic, representative government existed in many societies before it came to the U.S. government. One of the places where it was practiced was in the Muscogee Nation.

To look at the Muscogee and Poarch Creek governments of today, you might think that they were modeled after the modern U.S. government, but this would not be entirely true. In fact, in many ways, it was the other way around. When the European settlers rose up against the British *monarchical* government, they did not immediately know how they wanted their new government to run. What they did know was that they wanted to be able to make decisions for themselves without a person who was going to rule over them and tell them what to do.

One of the places the settlers looked when developing their new representative government was to Native people. Native governments, like that of the Muscogee Nation, had chiefs who served not as rulers but as representatives of the people. The chiefs were surrounded by councils of advisors and leaders, and all members of the community gathered together to voice their opinions and make important decisions. When a decision was

An engraving on this war memorial in Okmulgee, Oklahoma reads "Honor to all Muscogee Warriors." Muscogee people have served the United States in every American war.

made, it had to be agreed on by the whole community; the stronger or larger sections of the community could not overwhelm and disregard the opinions of the smaller portion of the community. Many of the positive, democratic features of our modern U.S. government were actually modeled after the government structures of tribes like the Muscogee Nation.

The Native people of North America are one of the smallest and historically most **oppressed** groups in the population of North America. Nevertheless, more Native Americans have served in the national armed forces than any other ethnic or cultural group. You may think that after all they have been through, the Muscogee people would no longer want anything to do with the United States, but this is not true. The Muscogee and Poarch people (as well as most Native people) are fiercely patriotic. At many homes, the American flag flies side by side with the flag of the tribe, and members of the Muscogee and Poarch people have served in every single military conflict since the Revolutionary War.

Mal D. McGhee is filled with enthusiasm for his work and his community. His life is a perfect example of how members from the Poarch tribe and Muscogee Nation contribute not only to their own communities but to the people of the United States as well. Growing up in Poarch, Mal had little opportunity for advanced education, but his elementary school teacher encouraged him to follow his dreams. Her husband was in the Air Force, and he told Mal about his life and travels. Mal developed a great interest in aircraft, and when he was old enough, he joined the armed forces where he served the United States and pursued his passion for aviation.

Mal's service, however, did not end when his military duties ended. Instead, he brought his success back to the Poarch Creek tribe, where he is now the general manager for Muscogee Metalworks and Manufacturing

Mal D. McGhee (center) and Timothy Ramer (left) inspect a new machine at Muskogee Metal Works/Manufacturing Technology, Inc. Mr. McGhee is the business's general manager. Mr. McGhee and Mr. Ramer both serve on the Poarch Creek Tribal Council.

Technology, Inc. He continues to serve his community and the United States by overseeing a business that creates hundreds of jobs and produces important hardware for the U.S. military. The materials produced in this facility in southern Alabama are now all over the world in the equipment that soldiers use to train, in the missiles of the armed forces, and even in nuclear submarines. Despite all of Mal's contributions, he does not see himself as pursuing personal success. Instead, he is pursuing the success and well-being of his community. All the work he does, he does for them.

Her brush glides strong and smooth across the white paper, and a woman's face appears. The woman's eyes have seen too much. Her body

Dana Tiger was recently inducted into the Oklahoma Women's Hall of Fame for her work as an artist and the many contributions she has made to society. She is the youngest woman ever to receive this honor.

Dana Tiger's artwork represents the strength, importance, and changing roles of women in Native society. The painting Women Drum *depicts women in a role that was traditionally held by men.*

This painting is another stirring example of Ms. Tiger's work. She has received numerous awards and often donates her time and talents to charitable causes.

has endured suffering. But her spirit shines with beauty and strength. The woman looking out from the brushstrokes on the paper does not merely survive in the challenges of her world; she battles, overcomes, and thrives, nursing others with her wisdom and healing the people with her dignity.

Today, the artwork of Dana Tiger is an unmistakable symbol of the strength of the Native people and the beauty of humanity. Working from her home in Oklahoma, Ms. Tiger's artwork depicts the women who have always been the foundation and caretakers of the Native people. Descended from the Creek, Seminole, and Cherokee people, Dana Tiger says,

"By realizing the natural strength and courage of women in my ancestry, I hope to portray the historical dignity and contemporary determination of Native American women."

The women in Dana's work are individuals who overcome adversity and make the world a better place through their struggles. Dana has known great adversity in her own life and knows how the fight to overcome makes the spirit grow. When Dana was just five years old, her father, Jerome Tiger, died in an accidental shooting. However, through the art he left behind, Dana's father remained alive to her. Today, like Dana's own work, Jerome Tiger's creations are considered some of the most important art to come from the Native community.

Later in life, Dana lost her brother when he was murdered. Not long after that, she suffered the devastating news that her sister had been diag-

Ms. Tiger has the unique ability to portray sorrow, strength, determination, and hope all in a single subject.

Holding On *by Dana Tiger.*

nosed with HIV, the virus that causes AIDS. Then, in 2000, Dana herself was diagnosed with Parkinson's disease, a condition that affects a person's nervous system and the ability to control the movement of her muscles. Despite these sorrows and challenges, Dana continues her work, realizing more than ever the importance of art in the world.

Dana uses her art to support many important organizations and causes. Many of her paintings have been sold as posters to benefit such things as the American Cancer Society, the AIDS Coalition for Indian Outreach, the American Indian College Fund, the National Organization for Women, and many other important causes. The significance of Ms. Tiger's work has been recognized with numerous awards. In 1998, she was honored with the Artist Choice and People's Choice Awards at the Colorado Indian Art Market. In 1999, she received Oklahoma State University's Leadership Legacy Award, and she was the recipient of the Spirit of Oklahoma Award at the Masters Art Show of the Five Tribes Museum in 1999 and again in 2001. Through the joy and knowledge it brings to people's lives and the money it raises for service organizations, Dana Tiger's artwork has touched and benefited people all over North America and the world.

Moving Forward *by Dana Tiger.*

Chapter 8

Concerns for Today, Hopes for the Future

The highway stretches across the Georgia landscape. It slices through once green fields and passes over river waters. The red clay lies naked and exposed beside the hot pavement, rolling on for miles. And then, the highway stops, hanging in the air, cut off in the middle of its construction, going nowhere.

Joyce Bear, the Cultural Preservation Officer of the Muscogee Nation can tell you a lot about this *arrested* highway and why the project stands momentarily abandoned. When it was discovered that the Georgia government had begun building a highway through some sacred Muscogee sites without researching the land or notifying the tribe, she played a large role in having its construction halted.

In 1990, the U.S. government passed the Grave Repatriation Act, giving Native people the right to preserve, restore, and protect many of the sacred sights that had been taken from them in the past. Part of Joyce Bear's job is to locate the sacred historic sites of her people and negotiate plans with the state governments for either preserving and protecting the sites or

The Poarch Creek Indian Princess is crowned at the annual Thanksgiving Pow Wow.

moving their contents to a place where they will remain safe for the future. One of the challenges she faces is the fact that most of the Muscogee Nation's sacred lands and sites are back in Georgia and Alabama, far from the tribe's present home. Before 1990, the tribe had little ability to protect these places. Today, much of Muscogee history lies at the bottoms of lakes created by dam projects, beneath farmer's fields and private citizens' homes, and bulldozed away by highway projects. Historic preservation is one of the most important concerns for the Muscogee people who wish to identify and protect all their sacred places, before their culture and history is lost.

Another important concern for both the Muscogee Nation and the Poarch Creek tribe is the environment. When the lands were seized from the Creek people, they were often treated badly by their new "owners." Now, as the Muscogee Nation and Poarch Creek tribe try to repurchase much of this land, they are inheriting the environmental disasters left by those who had the land before.

In Oklahoma, oil wells have had a devastating effect on the land and are the highest environmental concern. When the tribe seeks to purchase a new piece of land, it does a thorough environmental **assessment** of the area. Today, it is almost impossible for the Muscogee Nation to find a piece of property that does not have abandoned oil wells. These wells often release salt water and oil spills. Heavy metals, like mercury, **leach** from these wells into the ground water and cause illness and mental retardation in people. In order to purchase pieces of land, the tribe must promise to clean up any environmental problems on the property. The tribe would like to make all of the land clean again, but cleaning up such environmental disasters is

Joyce A. Bear is the Historic Preservation Officer of the Muscogee Nation of Oklahoma. Much of her work focuses on identifying Muscogee historical and sacred sites and then fighting to preserve them.

"Kill the Indian to Save the Child"

These words should make your blood run cold, but it was a sentiment still being heard all over North America as recently as fifty years ago. As if losing their land and tribal government hadn't been enough, Native parents in the United States and Canada then lost their children to federally sponsored, and often "religiously" run, Indian Schools. In these schools, Indian children literally had their heritage beaten out of them. When they were brought to the schools, they had their hair cut and their clothing taken away. They were dressed in school uniforms and punished severely if they spoke their Native language. Today, more than anything else, Indian boarding schools are to blame for the extensive, perhaps irreversible loss of language that has occurred in tribes all over North America.

extremely expensive. The tribe simply does not have the money that it would take to clean up the ruin left by oil companies and fortune seekers.

For the Poarch Creek tribe of Alabama, the most important environmental concern is the water. The Poarch Creek community lives at the beginning of a river that flows into the Gulf of Mexico. Because the river actually begins on their land, the Poarch tribe has great responsibility for the ***stewardship*** of the water and all the places it passes through on its way to the ocean. It is an enormous responsibility and one that tribal members take very seriously.

Georgia and Alabama used to be all ***wetlands*** and marshes. One of the first things settlers did when they came to the region was begin to drain these lands. Draining wetlands creates places for people to live, but it has disastrous effects on the environment. The Poarch Creek tribe now has numerous projects in which they are trying to restore the wetlands that naturally clean and purify the water. The tribe also hopes to one day build a water treatment facility so they will be able to oversee the cleansing of water used by the tribe.

One of the greatest hopes for the future of both the Muscogee Nation and the Poarch Creek tribe is to bring the language back to the communities

It is springtime in Alabama and the pecan trees will soon reveal their leaves. The Poarch Creek Tribe's pecan orchard is another agricultural project overseen by Perdido River Farms. The Poarch Creek Tribe's agricultural projects reflect their commitment to the environment and the land that has supported them for so long.

Poarch Creek school children proudly display their educational awards.

and the children. Today, there are no fluent speakers of the Mvskoke language in the Poarch tribe. They hope to someday create a program that brings fluent speakers from Oklahoma to Alabama where they can teach the tribal members their forgotten language.

Carrying on the language of their ancestors is a challenge for the Oklahoma people as well. Although there are still people who speak the Mvskoke language fluently, most of these people are now very elderly. When they die, all their knowledge will pass away with them, so people of the Muscogee Nation hope to learn as much as possible about their language and about themselves while there is still time. It is sometimes difficult, however, to get young people interested in their culture and in the language that their grandparents speak. Often, people do not realize the value of these things until they are older, and then it can be too late.

Wilbur Gouge, Speaker of the Muscogee Nation Council recognizes the extreme importance of language preservation in the tribe. "Language preservation is essential," he says, for it is language that identifies a nation. Today, many Muscogee people, like Mr. Gouge, realize that if they do not hold onto their heritage, the tribe will be lost. Like the earliest People, they may once more find themselves surrounded by fog, alone and separated from each other. But if they keep the language, stories, and traditions alive, the People will be able to reach out and support one another. And the Muscogee people will live forever.

Further Reading

Bruchac, Joseph. *The Great Ball Game: A Muskogee Story*. New York: Dial Books for Young Readers, 1994.

Grantham, Bill. *Creation Myths and Legends of the Creek Indians*. Gainesville: University Press of Florida, 2002.

Larrabee, Lisa. *Grandmother Five Baskets*. Niwot, Colo.: Robert Rinehart Publishers, 1993.

Lassieur, Allison. *Native Peoples: The Creek Nation*. Mankato, Minn.: Bridgestone Books 2002.

Lewis, David Jr. and Ann T. Jordan. *Creek Indian Medicine Ways: The Enduring Power of Mvskoke Religion*. Albuquerque: The University of New Mexico Press, 2002.

Scordato, Ellen. *The Creek Indians*. New York: Chelsea House Publishers, 1993.

Swanton, John R. *Creek Religion and Medicine*. Lincoln: University of Nebraska Press, 2000.

Wickman, Patricia Riles. *The Tree That Bends: Discourse, Power, and the Survival of the Maskoki People*. Tuscaloosa: The University of Alabama Press, 1999.

For More Information

Creek History
www.ourgeorgiahistory.com/indians/Creek

The Creek Nation–North Georgia's American Indians
www.ngeorgia.com/history/creek

The Muscogee Nation
www.ocevnet.org/creek

Muscogee Nation Genealogy
www.rootsweb.com/~itcreek

The Poarch Creek Tribe
www.poarchcreekindians.org

Publisher's Note:

The Web sites listed on this page were active at the time of publication. The publisher is not responsible for Web sites that have changed their address or discontinued operation since the date of publication. The publisher will review and update the Web sites upon each reprint.

Glossary

advantageous: Beneficial.

agriculturalists: People who support themselves through farming.

allotments: Individual sections of land.

apprentice: A person who studies under an expert in order to gain knowledge and experience, usually to learn a trade.

arbors: Open structures with a roof that provides shade.

arrested: Abruptly stopped or halted.

assessment: A test or review of something.

assimilation: Absorption into a new culture.

Bureau of Indian Affairs: The federal office that oversees Native Americans.

campaign platform: A set of issues that a person running for election promises to address if elected—the goals the candidate puts forth for his or her campaign.

cavalry: An army unit moving on horseback or motor vehicles.

civil: Relating to citizens, their relationships with each other, and their relationships with the government.

coerce: To use pressure, threats, or intimidation to force someone to do something.

communal: Something that is shared or held in common.

compensation: Something given as payment for a loss.

comprehensive: Covering broadly.

confederacy: A union of people, political parties, states, or governments.

conflagration: A huge and destructive fire.

conquistador: A Spanish soldier in the sixteenth century who strove to conquer the civilizations of the newly discovered Western Hemisphere.

constitution: The basic laws and principles of a nation or social organization.

continuity: The unbroken continuation of something from one place to another or from the past to the present.

contractors: People hired to do perform a service.

creation story: A specific type of story that tells how the world and life came to be.

criteria: The standards upon which a judgment is based.

curriculum: The course of study offered by schools.

democratic: Government of the people based on the principles of equality.

diplomatic: Using respect and sensitivity when interacting with others.

dire: Desperate.

disembowel: To tear the intestines and other organs in the abdomen out of the body.

disillusioned: Lost one's illusions about or enchantment with something.

diverse: Differing from one another or composed of different elements.

economies: Systems of production, development, and management of wealth.

encroached: Trespassed upon or secretly or gradually stole.

Head Start Program: A federally sponsored early education program for children whose families meet income guidelines.

inauguration: A ceremony installing someone into office.

indiscretions: Actions that are irresponsible or break social codes.

interrelations: Interactions between people.

leach: To seep from one place into another.

legislative: Relating to the creation of laws.

legitimate: Lawful or genuine.

lobbyists: People or groups who work to convince public officials to either support or deny a cause.

mandate: A command or order.

matrilineal: The tracing of ancestry and heritage through the mother's side of the family.

monarchical: Run by a king, queen, or other all-powerful leader.

negotiate: To discuss and arrange a mutual agreement.

neutrality: The refusal to take part in a war between other nations.

non-native: Not descended from any of the original inhabitants of the land in which one lives.

oil speculators: People who buy and sell oil, or land containing oil, for profit.

oppressed: Forcefully held down and denied freedom and success.

origin: The place from which something comes. The beginning.

pan-Indian: Across all Indian tribes, without tribal boundaries.

parceled: Given out in sections.

patents: Grants from the government giving people ownership of public lands.

perpetrator: The person responsible. One who commits a crime.

pervasive: Ever-present or permeating.

powwow: A celebration of Native American culture, tradition, and dance.

ratified: Adopted or signed into law.

rehabilitates: Restores to good condition.

relinquish: To give up.

relocation: The movement of one's home and life from one place and settling it into another location.

revered: Regarded with awe. Honored.

self-governance: Having an independent government with the ability to make decisions for itself.

stewardship: Serve as a caretaker.

subsidized: Supported with money from the government or an outside institution.

traditionalist: Someone who continues to believe, participate in, or honor the ways of the past.

transient: Staying in place for only a short time.

Union: The group of states that remained part of the United States during the Civil War.

watershed: A critical turning point.

Western Hemisphere: The half of the earth containing North America, Mexico, Central America, and South America.

wetlands: Lowland areas of marshes and swamps.

Index

Biographies

Autumn Libal is a graduate of Smith College. She is a freelance author and illustrator who lives in northeast Pennsylvania. She also authored *Folk Proverbs and Riddles*, in the Mason Crest series "North American Folklore," as well as several titles for "Psychiatric Disorders: Drugs and Psychology for the Mind and Body."

Benjamin Stewart, a graduate of Alfred University, is a freelance photographer and graphic artist. He traveled across North America to take the photographs included in this series.

Martha McCollough received her bachelor's and master's degrees in anthropology at the University of Alaska-Fairbanks, and she now teaches at the University of Nebraska. Her areas of study are contemporary Native American issues, ethnohistory, and the political and economic issues that surround encounters between North American Indians and Euroamericans.